4 Top Phonics Readers

W0018885

To the Shop!

Anne Taylor

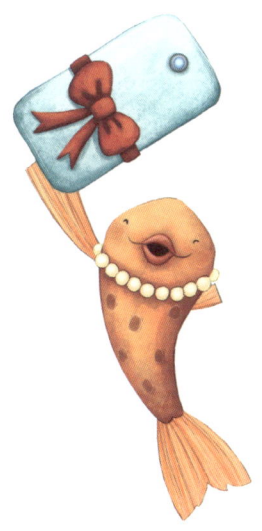

Seed Learning

Top Phonics Readers 4
To the Shop!

Anne Taylor

© 2017 Seed Learning, Inc.

Acquisitions Editor: Rose Morgan
Content Editor: Liana Robinson
Illustrators: Story 1 - Sandra Carmelo; Story 2 - Genie Espinosa;
　　　　　　Story 3 - James Murray; Story 4 - Laura Gonzalez
Design: Highline Studio

http://www.seed-learning.com

ISBN: 978-1-9464-5276-4

10 9 8 7 6 5 4 3 2 1
21 20 19 18 17

Contents

Story 1 The Sled 5

Story 2 Princess Tina's Treasure 13

Story 3 Ant's Tent 21

Story 4 To the Shop! 29

Word List 37

How to Use 39

The Sled

cl-, bl-, fl-,
gl-, pl-, sl-

Written by Anne Taylor

Illustrated by Sandra Carmelo

Dan looks at the clock.
It's ten. He wants to play.
Anna looks at the sky.
It's blue.

"Mom! Can we play with our sled?"
asks Dan.
"Please! We will go slow,"
says Anna.

"OK," says Mom.
"Wear your gloves.
Wear your hats.
And don't go by the cliff."

They are happy!
Anna claps her hands.
Dan's gloves are blue.
Anna's gloves are black.

They get their sled.
Dan and Anna slide down the hill.
It's fun!

"Our sled is a plane," says Dan.
"We can fly."
They have fun.

Dan and Anna eat plum slices.
"Did you go near the cliff?" asks Mom.
"No, not near the cliff," says Dan.

Princess Tina's Treasure

br-, cr-, fr-,
dr-, tr-, pr-

Written by **Anne Taylor**
Illustrated by **Genie Espinosa**

Tina is a brave princess.
She loves her pet frog.
He is her friend.
But she is sad. Her treasure is gone.

"Princess Tina," says Frog.
"I will help you find your treasure."

"The treasure is in a cave.
But there is a big dragon," says Frog.
"Let's go, Frog," says Tina.
"We must drive there," says Frog.

Tina puts on her blue dress.
She gets her brown truck.
Frog gets his trumpet.

"Look! It's Crab!" says Frog.
"Come on, Crab!" says Tina.
"Bring the drum, too," says Frog.

The friends go to the cave.
Frog blows his trumpet.
The dragon runs!
"Let's get the treasure," says Crab.

Crab and the princess fill the drum
with treasure.
"Thank you, Frog. Thank you, Crab.
Let's go home!"

Ant's Tent

sm-, sn-, st-, sw-,
-nt, -nk, -ng, -ck

Written by Anne Taylor

Illustrated by James Murray

Ant has a new tent.
The tent is pink.
He has a bag.
He puts snacks and sweets in it.

Ant shuts the door.
He puts a lock on it.
Ant smiles.
He is happy.

Ant sings, "La, la, la! Off I go
with my tent."
Ant steps on stones.
"One, two three!" he sings.

Ant stops.
He looks at plants and flowers.
He looks at swans on the lake.
What long necks they have!

Ant makes a fire.
"This is nice," he says.
"Swim with us," say the swans.

Ant swims.
But he smells smoke.
"Oh, no! My tent."

"You can sleep with us," say the swans.
"Thank you," says Ant.
But the swans snore all night!

To the Shop!

ch–, sh–, th–, ph–, wh–,
-ch, -sh, -th, -ph

Written by Anne Taylor

Illustrated by Laura Gonzalez

Wally is a white whale.
He lives in an old ship.
He swims all day.

One day, Wally Whale hears a whisper.

"Wally!"

"Hello?"

"Wally!"

"It's me, Lisa."

Lisa is Wally Whale's friend.
She is a thin fish. Lisa is rich.

"Let's go to the shops, Wally."

"OK, Lisa," says Wally Whale.
"I need a new phone."
"And then we can have pizza and chips for lunch,"
says Lisa.

"Let me brush my teeth,"
says Wally Whale.
"Let me wash my face.
Then we can go."

"What shop do you want to go to, Lisa?" asks Wally.

"This one!" says Lisa.

It is the phone shop.

"Let's take a photo with this new phone," says Lisa.
Wally smiles.
"This phone is for you, Wally," she says.
Wally smiles more!
"Thank you, Lisa!" he says.

Word List

Story 1

black

blue

clap

cliff

clock

fly

glove

plane

play

please

plum

sled

slice

slide

slow

Story 2

brave

bring

brown

crab

dragon

dress

drive

drum

friend

frog

princess

treasure

truck

trumpet

Word List

Story 3

 lock

 neck

 snack

 long

 sing

 pink

 ant

 plant

 tent

 smell

 smile

 smoke

 snore

 step

 stone

 stop

 swan

 sweets

 swim

Story 4

 chip

 lunch

 rich

 phone

 photo

 ship

 shop

 brush

 fish

 wash

 thank

 thin

 teeth

 whale

 whisper

 white

How to Use

The following are some ideas for ways to use the stories in this book.

Idea 1

- ★ Choose a story.
- ★ Look at the **Word List** for that story.
- ★ Find each word from the list in the story.
- ★ Then read the story.

Idea 2

- ★ Choose a story.
- ★ Look at the illustrations for the story.
- ★ Talk about the illustrations: Point and say the words you know in the illustrations.
- ★ Look for the words from the illustrations in the story while you read.

Idea 3

- ★ Choose a story.
- ★ Look at all the words with red letters in the story. Circle the words you know.
- ★ If you don't know a word, check the **Word List**.
- ★ Then read the story.
- ★ After reading, look at the words again. Can you remember the meaning of each one?

Idea 4

- ★ Choose a story.
- ★ Look at the illustration on each page: What do you see? What is happening?
- ★ Guess what you think the page will say.
- ★ Then read the page.
- ★ Repeat for every page of the story.